ICD-9-CM

for Physicians – Volumes 1 & 2

2015 | Expert

International Classification of Diseases
9th Revision
Clinical Modification
Sixth Edition

D0146963

Codes Valid October 1, 2014, through September 30, 2015

Publisher's Notice

All codes, indexes, and other material in the ICD-9-CM are compiled from official ICD-9-CM codes and instructions as well as the Medicare regulations and manuals issued or authorized by the Centers for Medicare and Medicaid Services. The code book is designed to provide accurate and authoritative information in regard to the subject covered, and every reasonable effort has been made to ensure the accuracy of the information within these pages. However, the ultimate responsibility for correct coding lies with the provider of services.

Optum, its employees, agents and staff make no representation, warranty or guarantee that this compilation of codes and narratives is error-free or that the use of this code book will prevent differences of opinion or disputes with Medicare or other third-party payers as to the codes that are accepted or the amounts that will be paid to providers for services, and will bear no responsibility or liability for the results or consequences of the use of this code book.

Our Commitment to Accuracy

Optum is committed to producing accurate and reliable materials. To report corrections, please visit www.optumcoding.com/accuracy or email accuracy@optum.com. You can also reach customer service by calling 1.800.464.3649, option 1.

Special Reports and Announcements

Purchase of this publication entitles you to Special Reports and announcements via email. Please call customer service at 800-464-3649 or contact your bookstore to take advantage of this exciting free service that will keep you abreast of important code changes and regulatory developments.

Review, download, and print the Special Reports in .pdf format. Log on to www.optumcoding.com/productalerts